A KID'S GUIDE TO THE

X Games

W9-BBJ-670

STREET LUGE

X in the Games

CHRISTOPHER BLOMQUIST

The Rosen Publishing Group's

PowerKids Press™

New York

For two Xtremely wonderful nephews, Timothy and James

Safety gear, including helmets, gloves, and racing suits with protective padding in the knees, elbows, and shoulders must be worn while street luging. Do not attempt to street luge without proper gear, instruction, and supervision.

Published in 2003 by The Rosen Publishing Group, Inc.
29 East 21st Street, New York, NY 10010

First Edition.

Editor: Nancy MacDonell Smith
Book Design: Mike Donnellan and Michael de Guzman
Photo Credits: Cover, pp. 4, 19 © Michael Zito/SportsChrome USA; p. 7 Mike Powell/Allsport; p. 8 © Kent Kochheiser/KKPhoto.net; p. 11 © Tom Hauck/Allsport; p. 12 © Jamie Squire/Allsport; pp. 15, 16, 21 © Icon Sports Media.

Blomquist, Christopher.
Street Luge in the X Games / by Christopher Blomquist.— 1st ed.
p. cm. — (A Kid's Guide to the X Games)
  ISBN 0-8239-6299-7 (library binding)
1. Street luge racing—Juvenile literature. [1. Street luge racing.] I. Title.
  GV859.82 .B56 2003
  796.6—dc21
                                                      2001006033

Manufactured in the United States of America

Contents

Street lugers race lying flat on their backs. Their boards don't have safety belts, so they have to hang on tight to keep from falling off!

What Is Street Luge?

In street luge a racer, or **luger**, lies faceup on a luge board, holds on to the sides of the board, and rides it downhill through a course that has many twists and turns. Luge boards are also called **sleds** or **rails**. They stand only 1 inch (2.5 cm) or so off the ground.

Lugers have to hold on tight! They can slide down the course as fast as 70 miles per hour (113 km/h), and their sleds do not have brakes. Instead lugers use their feet as brakes to control the sleds' speed.

Street luge is an **extreme sport**, because it's filled with risks and excitement. It's easy to get hurt in street luge. Lugers practice for a long time before trying any tricks. Another name for extreme sports is action sports, because they have so much action.

At every summer X Games, winning **athletes** are awarded **medals** and money. A gold medal is given to the first-place athlete. A silver medal is awarded for second place. A bronze medal goes to the third-place winner. At the 2001 X Games, more than $27,000 was awarded to the winning street lugers.

Street luge has been a men's sport at the X Games ever since the first summer X Games in Rhode Island in 1995. Bob Pereyra of California won the gold medal for the dual event, a race in which two lugers race on the track at the same time. After the 2000 X Games, the dual event was **discontinued**. Today there are just two X-Games luge events, the super mass event and the King of the Hill event.

Bob Pereyra won a gold medal in the first X Games for this run.

8

This luger is competing in the Red Bull Down Hill Extreme, one of the races in which lugers have to do well if they want to be part of the X Games.

How Lugers Get to the X Games

The **International Gravity Sports Association** (IGSA) is the group that **governs** street luge at the X Games. The IGSA decides which 30 lugers are invited to the X Games.

The top three finishers from each street luge event held at the most recent X Games are always invited back. Others **qualify** by doing well in four other luge races. These races are run each year in different parts of the world. The races are the Xtreme Grand Prix Super Mass, the Hot Heels Mass, the Red Bull Down Hill Extreme, and the Xtreme Grand Prix Last Chance Qualifier. The Xtreme Grand Prix events always take place in St. George, Utah. In addition to the qualifying lugers, four other lugers are invited to the X Games. These are lugers who the IGSA thinks are top racers.

Great X-Games Moments

During a practice run in 1998, Dennis Derammelaere, whose nickname is d-Rom, broke his leg. D-Rom almost did not qualify for the 1999 X Games in San Francisco, California, because of the injury. In 1999, though, d-Rom won the dual final against Lee Dansie of Renton, Washington. The race was so close that d-Rom's and Dansie's sleds locked together at one point! D-Rom says, "I edged Lee Dansie out at the finish line and won my first X-Games gold in front of my home crowd of nearly 20,000 people, and all my family and friends. The crowd **erupted**."

In 2000, there was another great luge **comeback**. Thirty-eight-year-old Bob Ozman of California had not even qualified for the 1999 games. Ozman won the gold medal in the 2000 dual race!

Bob Ozman is an X-Games gold-medal winner.
He's been luging for more than 25 years!

12

From left to right here are Dennis "d-Rom" Derammelaere, who won a silver medal, Biker Sherlock, who won the gold, and Lee Dansie, who won the bronze. They are at the 1997 X Games.

Star Lugers at the X Games

D-Rom is the current star luger at the X Games. He has won three gold medals, two silver medals, and two bronze medals. D-Rom has more X-Games medals than does any other street luger in history. Two of d-Rom's gold medals are for King of the Hill. This event decides who is the year's best luger. D-Rom won this event in 2000, the first year it took place, and in 2001. No one else has ever won King of the Hill!

Biker Sherlock of San Diego, California, is another great X-Games luger. Sherlock won four gold medals and one silver medal between 1996 and 1998. Sherlock sometimes teases the other athletes, so some lugers, such as d-Rom, do not get along with him. In fact Sherlock and d-Rom have been **rivals** for many years.

The Super Mass Event

In the super mass event, 24 riders race down a track. The track is lined with **bales** of hay to soften the blow if a rider crashes into the wall. Six athletes race on the track at a time. The three who get to the bottom the fastest advance to the next round. These rounds continue until only the six fastest athletes remain. In the last round these six athletes **compete** at once. The first-, second-, and third-place finishers in this race get medals.

At the 2001 X Games in Philadelphia, Pennsylvania, the lugers raced during a heavy rainstorm. The water made it hard for them to see. More than 2,000 wet fans watched 23-year-old Brent DeKeyser of California win the gold. It was DeKeyser's first X-Games medal!

Brent DeKeyser (center) is congratulated by other lugers after winning his first gold medal in the super mass event at the 2001 X Games in Philadelphia, Pennsylvania.

Despite the pouring rain, a big crowd turned out to watch the King of the Hill event at the 2001 X Games in Philadelphia, Pennsylvania.

The King of the Hill Event

King of the Hill is the X Games's newest street luge event. It was first raced at the 2000 X Games. This event decides who is the best luger of that year. Unlike other events, there is only one winner. He gets a gold medal. The second- and third-place finishers do not receive medals. So far d-Rom is the one and only "King of the Hill."

The athletes who compete in King of the Hill are gold medalists from years past and the gold and the silver medalist from the current year's super mass event.

The King of the Hill event is like the final round of the super mass event. Six lugers race on the track at the same time. Whoever crosses the finish line first wins.

Street Luge Equipment

To protect themselves from injury, all racers wear racing suits that are made either of leather or a special fabric called **Kevlar**. The suits are usually padded on the knees, the elbows, and the shoulders. IGSA rules also require that athletes wear a helmet and leather gloves.

The soles of the lugers' shoes are always made from rubber. Rubber helps the lugers to get a grip on the road when they use the shoes to brake.

"This sport is very serious and very dangerous, and is not to be taken lightly," says d-Rom. "There is a lot that one needs to learn about the sport before even thinking about trying it for the first time."

Street lugers wear helmets, leather gloves, special padded suits, and shoes with rubber soles to protect themselves when they race.

19

A Talk with Bob Ozman

What does it feel like to race in the X Games?
Participation in the X Games is really great . . . . The X Games is kind of like our **Olympics**. It is really neat to compete knowing that there are gold medals out there and thousands of people supporting us.

How have the X Games changed since you first raced in them in 1996?
At the very beginning of the X Games, it was kind of real small and there wasn't a whole lot of people. Over the years, I've seen the crowds grow.

How do you prepare for a run?
I train all year long and I try to ride at least twice a week. I go up to our local road which is 6.75 miles [11 km] long and has over 200 corners, and I do one full run. I also do push-ups, eat right, and drink lots of water.

Bob Ozman ▶

How did you first start street luging?
About 1975, I had some friends who took me up to this mountain road. They put me on a wooden water ski and said, "This is the road that we're going to go down!" I started riding then.

What is your favorite X-Games moment?
Winning my gold medal in 2000. For me to win a gold medal was . . . a dream come true.

What's Ahead for Street Luge

Street luge will be featured again at future summer X Games. Most lugers will probably welcome another chance to try to unseat d-Rom as "King of the Hill" or win a medal in the super mass event.

D-Rom himself thinks that street luge will continue to become more popular and to attract new riders and fans to the X Games.

"Street luge and the X Games will just continue to get bigger and bigger and you'll start to see younger, more talented riders pushing each other and the **veterans** doing the best that they can," d-Rom says.

Glossary

athletes (ATH-leets) People who take part in sports.

bales (BAYLZ) Large, square bunches of hay.

comeback (KUM-bak) The act of doing well again after having a period of not doing well.

compete (kum-PEET) To oppose someone else in a sports contest.

discontinued (dis-kun-TIN-yood) Stopped.

erupted (ee-RUPT-ed) Burst out with cheers.

extreme sport (ek-STREEM SPORT) A sport such as street luge, skateboarding, motocross, wakeboarding, bicycle stunt riding, and wakeboarding.

governs (GUH-vurnz) Sets the rules for.

International Gravity Sports Association (in-tur–NA-shuh-nul GRA-vih-tee SPORTS uh-soh-see-AY-shun) The group that sets the rules of street luge at the X Games.

Kevlar (KEV-lar) A brand of human-made fabric that is very strong and thick.

luger (LOO-zher) An athlete who races on a sled.

medals (MEH-dulz) Small, round pieces of metal that are given as awards.

Olympics (oh-LIHM-piks) The Olympic Games; an event at which the best athletes in the world meet every four years to compete against one another.

qualify (KWAH-lih-fy) To meet the requirements of something.

rails (RAYLZ) Luge boards.

rivals (RY-vulz) Two people who try to get or to do the same thing.

sleds (SLEDZ) Luge boards.

veterans (VEH-tuh-runz) People who have had their jobs for a long time.

Index

Web Sites

To learn more about street luge and the X Games, check out these Web sites:
www.dennisdRom.com
www.expn.go.com
www.streetluge.com